SCIENTIFIC AMERICAN. EDUCATIONAL PUBLISHING

CELEBRATE BOTANY!

10 FUN PROJECTS ABOUT PLANTS

BRING SCIENCE HOME

Published in 2024 by The Rosen Publishing Group, Inc.
2544 Clinton Street, Buffalo, NY 14224

Contains material from Scientific American, a division of Springer Nature America, Inc., reprinted by permission as well as original material from The Rosen Publishing Group.

Editor: Kelly Meredith
Designer: Rachel Rising

Activity on page 5 by Science Buddies/Svenja Lohner (May 2, 2019); page 11 by Science Buddies/Megan Arnett (December 15, 2016); page 17 by Science Buddies (August 13, 2015); page 24 by Science Buddies (August 6, 2015); page 29 by Science Buddies (May 9, 2013); page 35 by Science Buddies (March 14, 2013); page 41 by Science Buddies (August 16, 2012); page 45 by Science Buddies (July 19, 2012); page 51 (September 5, 2013); page 56 by Science Buddies (August 4, 2016).

All illustrations by Continuum Content Solutions

Photo Credits: pp. 4, 5, 11, 17, 24, 29, 35, 41, 45, 51, 56 nna Frajtova/Shutterstock.com; pp. 5, 8, 9, 11, 15, 17, 22, 23, 27, 32, 33, 35, 38, 39, 41, 43, 44, 45, 48, 54, 59, 60 cve iv/Shutterstock.com.

Library of Congress Cataloging-in-Publication Data

Names: Scientific American, inc., editor, issuing body.
Title: Celebrate botany!: 10 fun projects about plants / Scientific
    American Editors.
Other titles: 10 fun projects about plants | Bring science home.
Description: Buffalo, NY : Scientific American Educational Publishing, an
    imprint of Rosen Publishing, [2024] | Series: Bring science home |
    Includes index.
Identifiers: LCCN 2022057134 (print) | LCCN 2022057135 (ebook) | ISBN
    9781725349018 (library binding) | ISBN 9781725349001 (paperback) | ISBN
    9781725349025 (ebook)
Subjects: LCSH: Science projects--Juvenile literature. |
    Botany--Experiments--Juvenile literature. |
    Plants--Experiments--Juvenile literature.
Classification: LCC Q164 .C412 2024 (print) | LCC Q164 (ebook) | DDC
    580.78--dc23/eng20230203
LC record available at https://lccn.loc.gov/2022057134
LC ebook record available at https://lccn.loc.gov/2022057135

Manufactured in the United States of America

CPSIA Compliance Information: Batch #SACS24. For further information contact Rosen Publishing, New York, New York at 1-800-237-9932.

Find us on

CONTENTS

THESE ACTIVITIES INCLUDE
SCIENCE FAIR PROJECT IDEAS.

INTRODUCTION

Plants are some of the world's oldest—and most interesting—living organisms, with more than 8 million different kinds all over the globe. In these experiments, you'll replicate the changing seasons, count a variety of seeds, check out soil types, and learn more to help discover the power of plants.

Projects marked with include a section called "Science Fair Project Ideas." These ideas can help you develop your own original science fair project. Science fair judges tend to reward creative thought and imagination, and it helps if you are really interested in your project. You will also need to follow the scientific method. See page 61 for more information about that.

Dissect a Flower

A PETAL BY ANY OTHER NAME: BECOME A BUDDING BOTANIST BY LEARNING HOW EACH PART OF A FLOWER WORKS.

Springtime is when nature appears to come back to life after winter. Trees grow leaves, grass becomes green, and flowers sprout, displaying beautiful colors and sometimes spreading a delightful scent. But have you ever looked at a flower in more detail? What parts do flowers consist of? Are all flowers alike? In this activity you will find out by dissecting, or taking apart, a flower piece by piece. How many plant parts do you think you can identify?

PROJECT TIME
45 to 60 minutes

KEY CONCEPTS
Biology
Botany
Dissection
Plants
Reproduction

5

BACKGROUND

Plants that make flowers are known as flowering plants. But do flowers only exist to make plants look pretty? Not quite! Although they can be beautiful to us, flowers are made to attract pollinators for reproduction. This means the flowers are a crucial part of the process in growing seeds to make more plants. If you look closely at a flower, you might see that it is made of many different parts, each of which has a specific purpose.

Some flowering plants have a stem, which is a long stalk that carries water and nutrients and supports the flower. Leaves produce the food for the plant by photosynthesis, a process that helps makes plant food from light, carbon dioxide, and water.

When you look at the flower part of a flowering plant, the most obvious parts are probably the petals. They can vary in size and shape but are usually brightly colored. Their purpose is to attract the bees and other insects that help to pollinate the plants. You might be surprised to learn that some flowers—in the botanical world, they are called "perfect flowers"—have male parts and female parts, and each plays an important role during pollination.

The male parts, called stamens, look like long stalks (known as filaments) with a little round shape at their end called the anther, which contains the plant pollen. This bright yellow or orange dust is what insects carry from one plant to another. Pollination occurs if the pollen gets carried to the female parts of a new flower, called the pistil. The pistil is usually a long stalk located in the center of the flower and is also made up of several parts. Most importantly, it contains the ovary at its bottom, which houses the female plant eggs called ovules. When pollen is dropped into the pistil of a flower, the eggs, or ovules, inside the plant ovaries are fertilized. The fertilized ovules then grow into plant seeds, and the ovary becomes the fruit.

As you can see, a flower is much more than just beautiful to look at: it is essential for a plant to create more plants. Take a closer look at the many different plant parts in this activity and see how they differ from one flower to another!

MATERIALS

- Three different large fresh flowering plants, such as roses, tulips, lilies, petunias, carnations, or irises. You will need at least the stem with a flower attached for each of these. Note: Make sure you select "perfect flowers," which have male (stamen) and female (pistil) plant parts, such as those listed above. If you have allergies to certain plants, make sure that you use an alternative.

- Glass or cup with water
- Six paper plates
- Tweezers
- Scissors
- Magnifying glass or hand lens (optional)
- At least one additional (intact) specimen of each of the flower types you chose to dissect (optional)
- Paper (optional)
- Colored pencils (optional)
- Poster-sized paper or poster board (optional)
- Tape (optional)
- One or more vegetables or fruits, such as carrots, beets, asparagus, broccoli, cauliflower, tomatoes, apples, peppers, lettuce, peas, corn, or cabbage (optional)

PREPARATION

- Label each of the paper plates with one plant part ("Stem," "Petal," "Leaf," "Pistil," and "Stamen").

- Label one extra paper plate "Other."

- Draw lines onto each paper plate to divide it into three sections.

- Label each section on each plate with a name of one of the three flowering plants.

PROCEDURE

Carefully look at each of the flowering plants. If you have a magnifying glass, you can use it to examine your plants and their flowers. *What does each plant and flower look like?*

Choose one of your flowering plants, and start your plant dissection. Use your hands, scissors, or tweezers and carefully take apart your plant. *Which plant parts can you identify?*

- Once you have removed one part of the plant, try to identify it, and then place it on the corresponding plate. Put it in the section that is labeled with the right plant name. *Can you find a plant part for each plate?*

- If you cannot identify a specific plant part, place it on the "Other" plate.

- When you have finished taking the first plant apart, look at all its different parts. *How do different parts within one plant compare?*

- Next, repeat the dissection with the remaining two flowering plants. Then compare the plant parts on each paper plate. *What do you notice about the same plant part from different flowering plants?*

- Look at all the plant parts that you placed on the "Other" plate. *What do you think these plant parts are? How can you find out?*

ExTRA
If you have intact specimens of the types of flowers you dissected, examine these to see how all of the plant parts you identified fit together in the whole flower. *How do these vary across different types of flowers?*

ExTRA
Draw each of your flowering plants on a piece of paper. Color your plant and label each part that you identified.

ExTRA
Make a "plant parts" poster for each plant: Label a piece of paper with the name of one of your plants. Then tape the full flowering plant on one side of the paper. On the other side, tape each plant part into a different section of the paper. Label each plant part, and decorate your poster.

OBSERVATIONS AND RESULTS ·········

Just from looking at your flowering plants you might have noticed that each plant looks quite different. Obvious differences, for example, are the size or color of a flower. When you dissected the plants, however, you should have been able to identify the same plant parts for each of your plants. Each of them should have had a stem, which might have had some green leaves on it; colorful flower petals; the female flower part (pistil) at the center of the flower; and the male plant parts (stamen) that produce the pollen. When you compared each plant part, you might have noticed that they each look very different. A petal, for example, probably looked very different from the stem. This is because each plant part has a specific function, and its appearance is optimized to fulfill that function.

If you compare the same plant parts between different flowers, you might have observed that they looked somewhat similar. They might not have looked exactly the same, but you should have seen that they have the same functional features. Although flower petals can differ in size and color, they are usually brightly colored or shaped in a way to attract pollinators, such as bees. The differences between different flowering plants allow us to identify different plant species.

CLEANUP ·······························

You can put any remaining intact flowering plants into a jar or vase with water. Discard all the dissected flower parts in your compost or trash. Clean your work area, and wash your hands with water and soap.

Unlocking the Secrets of the Pine Cone

PINE CONES ARE SO IMPORTANT FOR PINE TREES BECAUSE THEY PROTECT THE SEEDS. SO WHAT DO THE CHANGING SEASONS DO TO A PINE CONE? TRY THIS EXPERIMENT TO LEARN MORE!

PROJECT TIME

 75 to 90 minutes

KEY CONCEPTS

Biology
Plant science
Temperature
Data

Depending on where you live, during the winter, the ground might be covered in snow, ice, and, most importantly, pine cones! We see pine cones everywhere during the winter—in wreaths, on trees, and in our yards. But did you know that pine cones have a vital job? They keep pine tree seeds safe and protect them from the freezing temperatures during the winter! To protect their seeds, pine cones can close their "scales" tightly, keeping out cold temperatures, winds, ice, and even animals that might eat their precious cargo. In this activity, we will observe how pine cones respond to different temperatures by mimicking changes in weather, all from our own kitchens! As an added bonus, after this activity, your pine cones will be ready to be added to your home as a holiday decoration or as a reminder of the plants of the season.

11

BACKGROUND

Did you know that pine cones can stay on pine trees for more than 10 years before falling to the ground? During that time, seeds for new pine trees grow under the scales of the pine cones. The scales protect the seeds from bad weather—and hungry animals. Eventually, however, the seeds need to be released so they can grow into new trees. To make sure they have the best chance of finding fertile soil and growing into trees, the pine cone scales stay tightly closed when the weather is inhospitable to new seed growth—that is, when it's very cold and damp outside. In contrast, when the weather is hot and dry, the seeds will have an easier time finding good soil for growing into trees. In these conditions, the pine cone scales will open, allowing seeds to escape and drift away to find new ground to grow into new trees!

As you will observe in this activity, after pine cones fall from the tree, they can still open and close; we will test the conditions that cause this—all from home!

MATERIALS

- At least three pine cones collected from outside
- An oven
- A large clear glass jar or bowl, large enough to hold about a cup of water
- A measuring tape
- Cold water
- A timer
- Tin foil
- A piece of paper
- Pencil or pen
- A baking tray
- A spoon or fork
- Permanent marker
- An adult helper
- Ice (optional)

PREPARATION

- With the help of an adult, preheat the oven to 250°F (121°C).

- Cover your baking tray with tinfoil.

- Fill up the glass jar with cold water (including a few pieces of ice if available).

- Use your permanent marker to label your pine cones. On the first one, write the letter "A." On the second pine cone, write "B" and on the third, write "C."

- On your paper, make three rows. Label the rows A, B, and C. Draw six columns. Label the columns "Initial Length," "Initial Circumference," "Cold Water Length," "Cold Water Circumference," "Final Length," and "Final Circumference."

PROCEDURE

Use your measuring tape to measure the length of each pine cone. For each pine cone, write down the length in the column "Initial Length." For all measurements in this activity, use centimeters (cm).

Use your measuring tape to measure the circumference of each pine cone at its widest point. For each pine cone, write down the circumference in the column "Initial Circumference."

Place pine cone A on the foil-covered baking tray. With the help of an adult, put the tray in the 250°F (121°C) oven.

With the help of an adult, check the pine cone every 10 minutes to make sure it doesn't burn. *Are the pine cones changing in any way as they get warmer? What do you notice about them as they get hot?*

While pine cone A heats up, place pine cone B in the cold water. Use your spoon to hold it underwater. Keep it there for two minutes. *What do you notice about the pine cone in the water? Does it sink or float? Why do you think this is true? Do you notice any changes as the pine cone sits in the cold water?*

Remove the pine cone from the cold water.

Use your measuring tape to measure the length of pine cone B. Write down the length in the column "Cold Water Length."

13

Use your measuring tape to again measure the circumference of pine cone B at the widest point. Write down its circumference in the column "Cold Water Circumference." Compare the length and circumference of pine cone B in each column. *Did its length or circumference change after you put it in cold water? If so, what kind of changes did you notice? Did it get larger or smaller? Do you notice any other changes about the pine cone? Does it look different? In what way?*

After pine cone A has been in the oven for 45 minutes, with the help of an adult, remove it from the oven. Allow it to cool until you can handle it comfortably.

Use your measuring tape to measure the length of pine cones A, B, and C. Write down their lengths in the column "Final Length."

Use the measuring tape to measure the circumference of pine cones A, B, and C at the widest points. For each pine cone, write down its circumference in the column "Final Circumference."

Compare the length and circumference of the pine cones for each column. If you like, you can use math to measure the changes using a few simple equations (and use the same equations to look for changes in length, by substituting length for circumference):

- o   Initial Circumference of Pine Cone A
- o   Hot Circumference of Pine Cone A
- o   Change Caused by Heat on Pine Cone A
- o   Final Circumference of Pine Cone A
- o   Initial Circumference of Pine Cone B
- o   Cold Circumference of Pine Cone B
- o   Change Caused by Cold on Pine Cone B
- o   Final Circumference of Pine Cone B
- o   Initial Circumference of Pine Cone C
- o   Change Caused by Control Conditions (air) on Pine Cone C
- o   Final Circumference of Pine Cone C

Using the data collected, determine which pine cone had the biggest change from the initial length and circumference. Notice which pine cone had the smallest change. *Why do you think some pine cones changed more or less than others? Do you notice any other changes in the pine cones? Do they look different? In what way?*

ExTRA

After pine cone A is out of the oven, try putting it into the cold water. Remove it after several minutes and measure its length and circumference again. *How does cold water affect the size and shape of the pine cones?*

ExTRA

Try the reverse. Take pine cone B from the cold water and place it into the oven to heat up. *What kind of impact does the heat have on the chilled pine cone? Is it similar to or different from the pine cone A, which was never in cold water?*

ExTRA

Try lowering the temperature of the oven to 150°F (65°C) and testing the effect on the size and shape of another pine cone. *Does it get larger than the one in the 250°F (121°C) oven—or smaller? Why do you think this happens?*

ExTRA

After taking the pine cones out of the oven and measuring, put them in the freezer overnight. When you take them out in the morning, measure their lengths and circumferences again and compare them with the final measurements. *Did the pine cones get larger or smaller? What other changes do you observe?*

OBSERVATIONS AND RESULTS ··········

   In this activity, you observed and recorded the effect of different temperatures and conditions on the size and appearance of pine cones. You might have noticed that placing pine cone B in the cold water caused its circumference to decrease. In response to cold and damp conditions, pine cone scales close tightly, making a natural shell to protect the seeds inside.

   After taking pine cone A out of the oven, you measured all of the pine cones to get their final measurements. When you compared the initial measurement of pine cone A, you should have observed that its circumference increased after being in the hot oven. The increase in the circumferences of the pine cones results from the scales of the pine cones opening up in response to the warmth of the oven. The pine cones think it's a warm summer day, and they are ready to release their seeds!

CLEANUP ···················

Turn off the oven. Dispose of the water in the sink. Return all other materials to where you found them in your home. Determine if you will reuse the pine cones as decorations. If not, return them to the outdoors.

Can Plants Help Slow Soil Erosion?

SOIL IS A SURPRISINGLY VALUABLE RESOURCE. BUT IT DOESN'T ALWAYS STICK AROUND. LEARN HOW A FEW PLANTS CAN HELP SAVE IT FROM BEING WASHED AWAY BY WATER.

PROJECT TIME

 60 to 90 minutes

KEY CONCEPTS

Soil erosion
Ecology
Geology

Perhaps you try to save water. Maybe you already reduce, reuse, and recycle. But have you ever considered conserving soil? Perhaps you haven't, but soil erosion—the wearing away of soil by water, wind, and other natural forces—can be a major ecological problem. Productive farmlands can disappear as nutrient-rich topsoil in fields washes away when heavy rains hit it. Waterways can then become polluted as pesticides and fertilizers wash into them. Even human life and property are jeopardized when soil erosion causes mudslides and landslides. The economic cost of soil erosion is estimated to be several billion dollars every year for the United States alone. This is a serious problem; can you help solve it? Do this activity and learn how to help save soil with nothing more than a few plants!

17

BACKGROUND

Soil erosion is partially caused by rain runoff washing away the soil. "Runoff" refers to the water that flows over soil's surface. It occurs when the soil is saturated, or unable to absorb more water.

One way to help combat soil erosion uses plants, which sometimes have extensive root systems that can help "grab on" to soil and keep it clumped together. You might have seen this if you've pulled a plant such as a weed or vegetable out of the ground and a clump of soil clung to its roots. Plants also help absorb some of the water in the soil. These effects make it harder for water to wash the soil away. Plants also help reduce erosion in other ways, such as breaking the wind that might blow dry topsoil away.

Now that you know more about soil erosion, let's see how rain contributes to water erosion.

MATERIALS

- Scissors or sharp knife (Have an adult help when using these implements.)
- Clean, empty 1-gallon (3.8 L) container with lid (such as a plastic milk jug)
- Water
- Two aluminum bread pans (Alternatively, you can use two sturdy shoe boxes that are similar in size. Make sure they are at least 2.75 inches [7 cm] deep.)
- Dirt (potting soil works well)
- Two aluminum 9-by-13-inch (22-by-33 cm) cake pans (Alternatively, you can use shallow plastic containers that are about 1 inch [3 cm] deep and wide enough for the short side of the bread pans or shoe boxes to rest in the containers.)
- 12 to 14 plastic forks
- Two blocks, shallow plastic containers, or other objects that can be used to prop up one edge of a bread pan to a height of roughly 1 to 2 inches

(3 to 5 cm) (Make sure both items are the same height and that these objects can get wet. Avoid using objects that shouldn't get wet, such as books.)
- Outdoor test area with a flat, level surface where it is easy to clean spilled water and soil.

You will likely spill water and soil in this activity. Be sure to protect your surface or use a surface that will not be ruined if it gets wet and dirty.
- Small gardening shovel, cake server, or spatula (optional)

PREPARATION ·····················

- Ask an adult to use the scissors or knife to poke one hole just above the handle of the 1-gallon (3.8 L) container. This hole will allow air to enter the watering can as liquid pours out. It can be quite big: 0.2 to 0.4 inch (0.5 to 1 cm) works well. (**Note**: If you have a watering can with a rain sprout that pours in many small rain-like streams, you can skip these steps and use the watering can to simulate rain.)

- Ask an adult to poke holes in the top of the container on the opposite side of the handle for the "rain" (water) to come out. Three rows of five holes each works well. These holes need to be a little smaller: about a 0.08-inch (2 mm) diameter works well. Do not worry if the holes are not exactly the same size or are not neatly organized in rows. You can test how it simulates rain and make adjustments if needed. *Do you think the number and/or size of the holes will change the type of rain you will create?*

- To test your watering can, fill it halfway with water and close the container. Over a sink or in an outdoor area that can get wet, tilt the can so water pours from the smaller holes. *Does it mimic rain well?* Play around with the angle at which you tilt the container. If water runs down the side of the container, tilt it more. If the rain comes out of the big hole as well as the little ones, you tilted the container too far. *What type of rain do you get: heavy downpour, steady rain, drizzle?* Make adjustments to the holes if needed. The goal is to mimic a steady, heavy rain.

19

- Fill the two bread pans with soil. While you do so, break up any clumps of soil that are present. Leave a little space at the top of the soil so runoff does not flow over the edges. The layer of soil should be at least 2.4 inches (6 cm) deep.

- Ideally, you would grow plants in one pan. That takes time! To complete this project more quickly, you will use plastic forks to simulate plants. The tines and curved area of the forks will simulate the root system.

- "Plant" forks in one box. Distribute the forks so the area is evenly covered. Plant the forks deep into the soil so the curved areas of the forks with the tines (pointy parts) are in the soil and only the handles stick out. Now remove the top half of one short side of each bread pan. To do so, use a small gardening shovel, cake server, spatula, or your hands to make two vertical cuts on one short side of a bread pan where it meets the longer sides, then fold down or remove a little over half of that short side to expose the soil. This will allow soil to flow out of the bread pan when you do your erosion test. Repeat this step with the other bread pan.

- Place a block (or object that can get wet) with a height of 1 to 2 inches (3 to 5 cm) next to an empty cake pan on your flat work surface. (The cake pan will collect eroded soil.)

- Place the "cut end" of a bread pan into the cake pan and push the block back until the other end of the bread pan rests on the block. The surface of the soil will be at an angle. This allows you to mimic a small slope like the slope of a hill. *Do you expect runoff to be a bigger problem on hillsides compared with flat surfaces?*

- Repeat the previous step with the other cake pan, block, and bread pan so you have two identical setups: one where the soil contains forks (substitute plants) and another with bare soil. Leave some space between the setups so spilled water and soil from one setup does not interfere with the other.

20

PROCEDURE

- Fill your watering container three-fourths full of water.

- Use your watering container to simulate rain over one bread pan or shoe box. Hold the watering container up high enough so rain falls on the entire width of the bread pan at once. If you are unable to cover the entire length of the bread pan at once, however, concentrate on its upper part. Be prepared—water will go to the sides of the pan and soil might splatter out of the pan, which is why you needed to protect your work surface. Make observations as rain comes down on the soil. *What happens first? Do you see changes in the soil surface? Do you see splats of soil? Does runoff (water flowing over the soil surface) occur instantly? Do you see a sudden change after a little while? Why do you think this change would happen?* Water this soil until the watering container is empty.

- Fill your watering jar three-fourths full again and use it to simulate rain in a similar way over the other bread pan or shoe box. Make sure you fill the watering container to a similar level, tilt the container in a similar way, and hold it at a similar height. *Why do you think this is important? Would changing these variables considerably simulate rain with a different intensity? Do you think the rain intensity influences the type and amount of erosion damage it causes?*

- Water the second bread pan or shoe box until the container is empty. *What do you observe this time? Do you see any differences between the two experiments?*

- Depending on the type of soil and size of your bread pans or shoe boxes, you might not see sizable erosion occur after the first downpour. If this is the case, fill you your watering jar halfway and simulate another downpour on your bread pans or shoe boxes, one at a time. If needed, repeat until you observe sizable erosion happening in at least one bread pan or shoe box. *Does erosion happen after the same amount of rain for both setups?*

To see the amount of eroded soil in your cake pan, slightly tilt the cake pans (one at a time) to drain the water. Some soil suspended in the water will drain out with it but the majority of the eroded soil will settle to the bottom and stay in the pan.

Compare the amount of eroded soil collected for both experiments. *Do you find more, less, or equal amounts of eroded soil?*

How do you think forks are similar to small plants? How do you think they are different? Do you think having small plants in the bread pan or shoe box would have helped reduce erosion even more?

How do you think real-world situations might be similar to or different from your test?

⚛ SCIENCE FAIR IDEA

Try this experiment with different soil types.
Are some more susceptible to erosion than others?

⚛ SCIENCE FAIR IDEA

Grow radish sprouts or other fast-growing plants in a bread pan. Redo the test, now comparing bare soil with soil covered with sprouts. Be sure to use a bread pan for this; a cardboard shoe box will soften when filled with moist soil for a longer time. *Would plant sprouts used in this test be a good substitute for full-size plants or trees in real situations? Which one do you expect to hold soil best—forks, sprouts, or full-grown plants?*

EXTRA

Look up more details about the different types of water erosion. Sheet, rill, gully, and splash are some examples. *What type of erosion do you observe during your experiment?*

OBSERVATIONS AND RESULTS · · · · · · · · ·

Did you find more soil was washed away from the bread pan or shoebox filled with bare soil? Initially, you might have seen that the impact of heavy raindrops falling on the soil causes pieces to break away, leaving little dips. Maybe you observed soil splatting away as a result.

At the start, the soil could probably absorb most of the rain. It acts like a sponge, holding the water. With a prolonged downpour, however, the soil is not always able to absorb the water fast enough and you likely observed excess water starting to flow on top of the soil. Sooner or later you should have observed excess water flowing down, as the soil becomes saturated and could not absorb more water.

The water flowing on top of the soil is called runoff. As it flows, it carries loose soil with it. The amount of soil transported depends on the speed and volume of the flowing water as well as the type of soil and its slope. Although forks cannot hold on to soil as well as plants do, they do help hold it together and ward off larger layers of soil sliding down. As a result, you probably collected more eroded soil from rain falling on the bare soil.

CLEANUP ·

You can reuse the soil from this activity for planting potted plants, starting seedlings, or (with permission) adding to soil outside.

The soil might be too saturated to use right away; if this is the case, try letting it dry out for a day or more before reusing it. Don't forget to recycle your homemade watering can if you have this ability where you live—or continue to use it to water your own plants!

Gone with the Wind
Plant Seed Dispersal

SCATTERING SEEDS! LEARN HOW SOME OF THE MOST FUN SEEDS OF SUMMER TRAVEL SO WELL ON THE BREEZE. CAN YOU DESIGN A SEED THAT SCATTERS WELL WITH THE WIND?

Have you ever looked outside on a windy day and seen "helicopter" seeds spinning through the air? Or picked up a dandelion and blown on it, sending the tiny, fluffy seeds flying all over the place? Wind is very important for dispersing seeds to help plants reproduce. In this project, you will design some of your own "seeds" and see which ones work best when they are blown across the room by a fan.

PROJECT TIME

45 to 60 minutes

KEY CONCEPTS

Biology
Plants
Evolution
Aerodynamics

24

BACKGROUND

Dispersal of seeds is very important for the survival of plant species. If plants grow too closely together, they have to compete for light, water, and nutrients from the soil. Seed dispersal allows plants to spread out from a wide area and avoid competing with one another for the same resources.

Seeds are dispersed in several different ways. In some plants, seeds are housed within a fruit (such as apples or oranges). These fruits, including the seeds, are eaten by animals who then disperse the seeds when they defecate. Some fruits, such as coconuts, can be carried by water. Some seeds have little hooks that can stick on to an animal's furry coat. (You may get them stuck on your clothing if you ever go hiking in the woods or tall grass.)

Other seeds are dispersed by the wind. This includes the "winged" seeds from a maple tree that spin and "helicopter" through the air as they fall or the light feathery seeds from a dandelion that can catch on a breeze. The longer a seed stays in the air, the farther it can be blown by the wind, helping the plant species widely scatter its offspring. In this project you will make your own artificial "seeds" from craft materials. Can you design seeds that will stay in the air for a long time?

MATERIALS

- Examples of different seeds that are dispersed by the wind (Depending on where you live, you may be able to find some of these seeds outside. If you have access to the internet, you can also do a web search for maple seeds, dandelion seeds, and other types of wind-dispersed seeds to get ideas.)
- Small, uniform, lightweight objects that you can use as "seeds" (For example, you could use small paper clips or small binder clips. Or you could purchase a bag of real seeds—such as sunflower seeds—at the supermarket.)
- Craft supplies to build dispersal mechanisms for your seeds (These could be as simple as paper and tape, or you could also use things such as streamers, cotton balls, or items you find outside, such as blades of grass.)

- Scissors, tape, and glue for cutting and attaching your craft supplies to your seeds (Be careful when using scissors.)
- A window fan or large box fan (Use with caution and appropriate supervision.)
- Stopwatch or timer (optional)
- Measuring tape or ruler (optional)

PREPARATION

- Clear an open area in the room where you will do the seed-testing activity.

- Place the fan on a table or chair, aimed across the room. You can also do the experiment outside on a windy day.

PROCEDURE

Design and build several—at least four—dispersal mechanisms for your seeds. The activity works best if you can create at least two similar dispersal mechanisms to test against one another (see examples below). You can use your imagination and come up with your own ideas, but here are a few to get you started (using a paper clip as an example "seed"):

o Attach a paper clip to a small, square piece of paper, about the size of a sticky note, without making any changes to the paper.

o Attach a paper clip to another small piece of paper, but make several parallel cuts in one side of the paper to give it "frills" and bend them outward.

o Attach a paper clip to a cotton ball.

o Attach a paper clip to a cotton ball that you have pulled on to expand it a bit and make it wispier.

o   Cut out some paper in the shape of a maple seed and attach a paper clip.

- Which seed dispersal mechanism or mechanisms do you think will travel the farthest when dropped in front of the fan? Why?

- Turn on the fan. Standing in the same place, try dropping your seeds one at a time in front of the fan. Also try dropping a plain "seed" (for example, a regular paper clip with nothing attached) to see what happens.

- How far do the seeds get blown by the fan? Do certain seeds take longer to reach the ground than others?

- Think about your results. Did some of your designs not work at all (fall straight down, without blowing forward)? Did some work better than others? What can you do to improve your designs? Can you make changes to your seeds to make them blow even farther?

ExTRA

Have a friend use a stopwatch to time how long it takes the seeds to hit the ground. This might be easier if you drop the seeds from a higher location. (Have a tall adult drop them, carefully stand on a chair, or drop them from the top of stairs.)

ExTRA

Use a tape measure to record how far the seeds travel horizontally from where you drop them to where they hit the ground. Which seeds go the farthest?

ExTRA

How do your results change if you change the speed of the fan?

OBSERVATIONS AND RESULTS ············

You should find that adding light materials to the "seed" can make it fall more slowly and blow farther. However, the shape of the materials is also very important. For example, a paper clip attached to a crumpled-up piece of paper will still fall very fast. A piece of paper with a "wing" design (similar to that of a maple seed) or a bunch of individual streamers (like a dandelion seed), however, will fall more slowly and be blown farther by the fan. Exactly how far the seeds blow will depend on the strength of your fan, but you should definitely see a difference in the horizontal distance traveled between a "plain" seed and one with a dispersal mechanism. When you take your best designs and try to improve on them, you mimic the process of evolution—because the "best" seed designs in nature are the ones most likely to reproduce!

CLEANUP ·······················

Throw away or recycle seeds. Return the other materials to where you found them in your home.

Springtime Science
Exploring the Pigments in Flowers

FLOWERS COME IN A VARIETY OF COLORS. WHAT CAUSES FLOWERS TO BE A CERTAIN SHADE? FIND OUT WITH PAPER CHROMATOGRAPHY!

PROJECT TIME

3 to 4 hours

KEY CONCEPTS

Chemistry
Pigments
Flowers
Plant biology

In the springtime, it can be easy to spot flowers in a dazzling array of colors at flower gardens and in plant nurseries. And when Mother's Day is near, stunning flower bouquets seem to be everywhere. Have you ever wondered what makes a flower appear a certain color to us? For example, what pigments make a rose a deep, rich shade of red? Do different flowers use the same pigments? In this activity, you'll get to use paper chromatography to investigate if the pigments from one type of red flower are different from those in another type of red flower.

29

BACKGROUND

A flower's pigments help to attract possible pollinators, such as honeybees, butterflies, and hummingbirds. There are two major classes of flower pigments: carotenoids and flavonoids. Carotenoids include carotene pigments (which produce yellow, orange, and red colors). Flavonoids include anthocyanin pigments (which produce red, purple, magenta, and blue colors). Usually, the color a flower appears depends on the color of the pigments in the flower, but this can be affected by other factors. For example, blue cornflowers have the same pigments as red roses, but the pigments in the cornflower petals are bound to other pigments and metal ions, making cornflowers look blue.

In this activity, you'll use paper chromatography to investigate the pigments in flowers. Chromatography is a technique that is used to separate the components of a complex mixture or solution. In paper chromatography, a solution is dabbed onto the bottom of a paper strip, and the strip is then placed in a liquid. The liquid moves up the paper and, depending on how soluble they are in the liquid, the pigments are carried up the paper with the moving liquid. Ideally the components move at different speeds, so they can be separated.

MATERIALS

- Paper towels (Thicker ones will work better.)
- Scissors
- Pencil
- Ruler
- Jar, drinking glass, or mug
- Measuring cup
- 70 percent isopropyl rubbing alcohol
- Water (Distilled water is preferable, but tap water is also suitable.)
- Large-mouth glass jar
- Red flower petals. Try to get at least two flower petals from at least three different plants, such as from your own garden, a florist, or plant nursery. You could also try flowers that are similar in color, such as more purple or orange flowers. (Pink petals may not work well.) Larger petals, such as those from roses and tulips, work better than smaller petals.
- Piece of scratch paper
- Coin
- Timer or clock

PREPARATION

- Cut the paper towels into strips that are each about 1 inch (2.5 cm) wide. Make each strip the same height as your large-mouth glass jar. Cut at least one strip for each type of flower you want to investigate.

- Draw a pencil line 1 inch (2.5 cm) from the bottom end of each paper strip.

- At the other end of each paper strip, use a pencil to label which flower will be spotted on the strip.

- In a clean jar, drinking class, or mug, mix 1/4 cup (59 ml) of water with 1/4 cup (59 ml) of the isopropyl rubbing alcohol. Pour a small amount of this mixture into the large-mouth glass jar, a little less than 1 inch (2.5 cm) deep. Having an adult nearby is recommended when working with the rubbing alcohol.

PROCEDURE

Place a piece of scratch paper on a hard, flat surface. (Some pigments can stain so you will want to protect the surface with this piece of scratch paper.) Put one of the paper towel strips on top of the piece of scratch paper. Lay a flower petal on the paper strip, over the line you drew.

Roll a coin on its edge, like a wheel, over the petal and across the pencil line. Push down hard so that the petal is crushed and a strip of pigment is visibly transferred to the paper towel strip. Repeat this about three or four times (using a fresh part of the petal each time) so that a thick line of pigment is transferred to the pencil line. *How does the line of pigment look? Is it what you expected?*

OBSERVATIONS AND RESULTS ··········

Did you find that most (or all) of the red flowers used the same pigments? Did the pigments create a reddish-purplish band on the paper towel strips?

Carotene pigments (which are carotenoids) produce yellow, orange, and red colors, whereas anthocyanin pigments (which are flavonoids) produce red, purple, magenta and blue colors. Most red flowers use anthocyanin pigments to produce their red coloring (although some use carotenoids). On the paper strips, the anthocyanin pigments may have appeared as a purplish-reddish band. If different red flowers made similarly colored bands around the same height on the paper towel strip as one another, then they likely have the same pigment. If the bands are different colors and/or at different heights, however, then they're probably different pigments. Carotene pigments are more commonly found in vegetables, and, in fact, they are what make carrots look orange. Yellow and orange flowers can have carotenoids or flavonoids, and blue flowers often have anthocyanin pigments that are modified. Some flowers even have chlorophyll that gives them green coloring.

In paper chromatography, the pigments move up the paper with the liquid and are separated based on the solubility of the pigments. So, if a pigment is very soluble in the diluted isopropyl rubbing alcohol, it should be easily carried far up the paper strip, whereas a less soluble pigment will generally travel a shorter distance. Because different pigments often have different solubilities, they can be separated from one another on the paper strip.

CLEANUP ·····················

Throw away paper towel strips and used flower petals. Dump water and rubbing alcohol mixture down the drain. Return the other materials to where you found them in your home.

Sci-Fi Science
Attack of the Cabbage Clones

SEEING DOUBLE? FIND OUT HOW YOU CAN CREATE MORE PLANTS IN THIS CLONING EXPERIMENT!

Around Saint Patrick's Day, the color green seems to be everywhere—from hats to shamrocks. For this Saint Paddy's Day, you could show off your own green creation by cloning a plant! Many sci-fi tales of cloned organisms have been based on the actual scientific method for cloning animals or plants. In the real world, the cloning of plants is often used in modern agriculture. How do you clone a plant? In this activity, you will get to find out by making your own cabbage clones!

PROJECT TIME
at least 7 days

KEY CONCEPTS
Plant biology
Cloning
Reproduction
Asexual reproduction

35

BACKGROUND

Unlike most animals, plants commonly use two different ways to reproduce, depending on conditions. These two different types of reproduction are sexual reproduction and asexual reproduction. Many plants we're familiar with, such as flowering plants, undergo sexual reproduction by making seeds, where each seed contains an embryo that will grow into a mature plant under the right conditions. Sexual reproduction requires both male and female parts of a plant, which mix to form the embryo, bringing different sets of genes from both parent plants.

Asexual reproduction in plants is when new plants are made without male and female parts mixing, and it can be done without making seeds. The new progeny plant is a genetic clone of the parent plant. Although asexual reproduction usually produces plants with relatively less diversity compared with those created via sexual reproduction, asexual reproduction can be quite useful. Cloning plants is very common in agriculture because a plant can often be made relatively quickly this way, and it allows a farmer to grow more reliable produce, harvesting essentially the same plant from one year to the next.

MATERIALS

- Three paper towels
- Three small, sealable plastic bags
- Scissors (optional)
- Water
- Fresh head of cabbage. Napa cabbage is recommended, because it is longer than the more common round cabbage, is less dense, easier to pick apart, and has a longer stem.
- Cutting board
- Knife
- Camera (optional)
- Permanent marker

PREPARATION

- Fold a paper towel in half and then fold it in half again so that it can fit into a sealable plastic bag. Slip the folded paper towel into the bag so that the last fold you made is at the bottom of the bag. (If the folded paper towel is too long to fit into the bag, trim it to fit using scissors.)

- Add water to the bag so that the paper towel is damp, but do not add so much water that it is dripping wet. Pour out any extra water.

- Repeat these steps with the other paper towels and sealable plastic bags so that you have prepared three sealable plastic bags with damp paper towels inside.

- Remove the leaves from your cabbage. Beginning with the outer leaves, gently pull all of the leaves of the cabbage off the stem. Do not worry if you don't get the entire leaf removed. It is better to leave some of the leaf attached than to risk damaging the stem.

- You should have an adult's help to use the knife when cutting the stem in the procedure.

PROCEDURE

Place the cabbage stem on a cutting board and, with an adult's help, use a knife to carefully slice the stem crosswise into three pieces. Try to make each piece about the same length. You should have a top, middle, and bottom piece, where the bottom piece would be closest to where the roots were (they should already have been removed) and the top piece would be at the top of the plant. *How are the pieces different from each other? How are they similar? What color(s) are they?*

If you have a camera handy, you can take pictures of the stem pieces.

Put one stem piece into each bag you have prepared. Put each piece in the middle of the folded layers of the paper towel (with two layers above the piece and two below it). Blow a tiny bit of air into each bag before sealing it.

Once sealed, use the permanent marker to label each bag (as "top," "middle," or "bottom") based on which piece is inside.

- Place the three bags near a window at room temperature.

- The next day, open the bags and observe the cabbage stem pieces. *Do the pieces seem to have changed? Do some look like they're becoming clones? How can you tell?*

- Reseal each bag, again blowing a tiny bit of air into each one before doing so. Place the bags back near the window.

- Continue observing the cabbage stem pieces each day like this until you have observed them for at least a week. *How do the pieces change over time? Do some pieces sprout green leaves or develop small green spots? Do some seem to rot—turning brown, slimy, and smelly?*

- Did one piece (top, middle, or bottom) become the best clone? How can you tell? Did a certain piece not clone at all? If some pieces became better clones than others, why do you think this is?

ExTRA

You can try to continue growing the clones you started in this activity. To do this, remove the clones from the bags after they've been growing for about 10 to 12 days. Have an adult help you carefully use a knife to cut off and discard any rotting pieces, and put the clones onto damp potting soil in a pot or another container. Keep the soil damp and observe how the clones grow and change over time. *Do the leaves grow? Do they sprout roots? Do they turn into plants like the original cabbage you used or are they different somehow?*

SCIENCE FAIR IDEA

You can try cloning other crops as well, such as celery stem parts, tubers of potatoes, slices of carrot, lettuce stems, separated garlic cloves, etcetera. *Do clones come from the same part of the plant? Do other crops need different conditions to be cloned? Are some crops cloned much more easily than others?*

OBSERVATIONS AND RESULTS ·········

Did the top stem piece grow green leaves and overall make a much better clone than the middle or bottom pieces? Did the middle piece grow at least a few small green spots, whereas the bottom had fewer green spots—if any?

When you cut the stem into three pieces, you probably saw that all three pieces had some leaves growing from them, which you could see by the leaf stubs left from when you removed the leaves. The piece that should have had the most leaves was the top piece, the only piece that had leaves on its top side. This is relevant because plants have a type of tissue called the meristem, which is where plants can sprout and is thereby important for asexual reproduction. Meristem tissue is usually in the plant's root tips (which had been removed from the cabbage) and the stem's tip, where it grows the stem, new leaves, and buds. You should have seen that after only a day, the top piece looked greener than it had after you removed its leaves—and it became greener each day, growing several leaves mostly from the top of the piece. By the time the week was over, the middle piece should have sprouted a few small green spots where the leaves meet the stem. The bottom piece may have sprouted a few green spots as well, but it probably had rotted much more than the other pieces.

CLEANUP ·······················

Because you did not need the cabbage leaves for this activity, you could use them to make a cabbage soup or coleslaw. You can also continue trying to grow your clones in soil or compost them.

39

Staining Science
Capillary Action of Dyed Water in Plants

WHAT HAPPENS TO WATER WHEN YOU GIVE IT TO A PLANT? GRAB A FEW CARNATIONS, AND LET'S FIND OUT!

Have you ever heard someone say, "That plant is thirsty?" Or "Give that plant a drink of water"? We know that all plants need water to survive, even bouquets of cut flowers and plants living in deserts. But have you ever thought about how water moves within the plant? In this activity, you'll put carnations in dyed water to figure out where the water goes. Where do you think the dyed water will travel, and what will this tell you about how the water moves in the cut flowers?

PROJECT TIME

2 to 5 days

KEY CONCEPTS

Plant biology
Capillary action
Water
Dyes
Colors

41

BACKGROUND

Plants use water to keep their roots, stems, leaves, and flowers healthy and to prevent them from drying and wilting. The water is also used to carry dissolved nutrients throughout the plant.

Most of the time, plants get their water from the ground. This means a plant has to transport the water from its roots up and throughout the rest of the plant. How does it do this? Water moves through the plant by means of capillary action. Capillary action occurs when the forces binding a liquid together (cohesion and surface tension) and the forces attracting that bound liquid to another surface (adhesion) are greater than the force of gravity. Through these binding and surface forces, the plant's stem basically sucks up water—almost like drinking through a straw!

A simple way of observing capillary action is to take a teaspoon of water and gently pour it in a pool on a countertop. You'll notice that the water stays together in the pool, rather than flattening out across the countertop. (This happens because of cohesion and surface tension.) Now gently dip the corner of a paper towel in the pool of water. The water adheres to the paper and "climbs" up the paper towel. This is capillary action.

MATERIALS

- Water
- Measuring cup
- Glass cup or vase
- Blue or red food coloring
- Several white carnations (at least three). **Tip:** Fresher flowers work better than older ones
- Knife
- Camera (optional)

PREPARATION

- Measure 1/2 cup (118 ml) of water and pour it into the glass or vase.

- Add 20 drops of food coloring to the water in the glass.

- With the help of an adult, use a knife to cut the bottom stem tips of several (at least three) white carnations at a 45-degree angle. **Tip:** Be sure not to use scissors; they will crush the stems, reducing their ability to absorb water. Also, shorter stems work better than longer ones.

- Place the carnations in the dyed water. As you do this, use the stems of the carnations to stir the water until the dye has fully dissolved.

PROCEDURE

Observe the flowers immediately after you put them in the water. If you have a camera, take a picture of the flowers.

Observe the flowers 2, 4, 24, 48, and 72 hours after you put them in the dyed water. Be sure to also observe their stems, especially the bumps where the leaves branch from the stem and are lighter green (it may be easier to see the dye here). If you have a camera, take pictures of the flowers and stems at these time points.

How did the flowers look after 2 hours? What about after 4, 24, 48, and 72 hours? How did their appearance change over this time period?

What does the flowers' change in appearance tell you about how water moves through them?

⚛ SCIENCE FAIR IDEA

In this activity, you used carnations, but do you think you'd see the same results with other flowers and plants? Try this activity with another white flower— a daisy, for instance—or a plant that is mostly stem, such as a stalk of celery.

⚛ SCIENCE FAIR IDEA

Try doing this activity again but use higher or lower concentrations of food coloring, such as one-half, twice, four times, or 10 times as much; be sure to mix each dye amount with the same amount of water. *What happens if you increase or decrease the concentration of food coloring in the water?*

EXTRA

How would you make a multicolor carnation? **Tip:** You could try (1) leaving the flower for a day in one color of water and then putting it in another color of water for a second day or (2) splitting the end of the stem in two and immersing each half in a different color of water.

OBSERVATIONS AND RESULTS ··········

When you put the flowers in the dyed water, did you see some of the flowers start to show spots of dye after 2 hours? Did you also see some dye in the stems? After 24 hours, did the flowers overall have a colored hue to them? Did this hue become more pronounced, or darker, after 48 and 72 hours?

Water moves through the plant by means of capillary action. Specifically, the water is pulled through the stem and then makes its way up to the flower. After 2 hours of being in the dyed water, some flowers should have clearly showed dyed spots near the edges of their petals. The water that has been pulled up undergoes a process called transpiration, which is when the water from leaves and flower petals evaporates. However, the dye it brought along doesn't evaporate, and stays around to color the flower. The loss of water generates low water pressure in the leaves and petals, causing more colored water to be pulled through the stem. By 24 hours, the flowers should have gained an overall dyed hue, which darkened a little over time. The stems should have also become slightly dyed in places, particularly where the leaves branch off.

CLEANUP ···················

Display the flowers until they are wilted, then compost them or throw them away.

Seminal Science
How Many Seeds Do Different Fruits Produce?

BIG, LITTLE, ROUND, LONG—DOES THE SHAPE OR SIZE OF A FRUIT CHANGE THE NUMBER OF SEEDS? GRAB SOME OF YOUR FAVORITES TO FIND OUT!

Do you like your strawberry jelly with or without the seeds? Are you glad to have a seed-free watermelon, or do you enjoy spitting the seeds into a garden? You might not like finding seeds in your fruit, but fruit is a plant's tool for dispersing seeds to create offspring. In this activity, you will investigate how many seeds can be dispersed for each type of fruit. Based on the number of seeds they produce, how productive do you think some of your favorite fruits are?

PROJECT TIME
45 to 60 minutes

KEY CONCEPTS
Plants
Fruits
Seeds
Flowers
Biology

45

BACKGROUND

Many plants grow fruit to enclose and protect their seeds, which need to spread out to grow new plants. Animals love to eat sweet, juicy fruit. This approach would seem like a poor way for plants to protect their seeds, so why would making fruit that is tasty be beneficial? When an animal eats fruit, the fleshy part is digested. The seeds, however, pass without harm through the digestive system and are spread by the animal when it excretes (poops). In this way, they are deposited farther from the original plant (along with a little bit of fresh fertilizer) and can grow into a new plant. This is called seed dispersal, and it is just one strategy that plants use to spread seeds over a wide area and make more plants.

You might think that all fruit-bearing plants would pack as many seeds as possible into each fruit to maximize the number of new plants that will grow. But, in fact, different plants have different strategies for seed production and dispersal. Some fruits produce many, many seeds to make sure that at least some will grow, even if most fail. Other fruits put all of their resources into producing and protecting one very large seed.

MATERIALS

- Different types of fruits: Try to include a pepper, tomato, and apple as well as a squash or cucumber (Yes, all of these are technically considered the "fruits" of their plants.)
- Knife
- Cutting board
- Paper towels

PREPARATION

- Go to the grocery store and pick out different kinds of fruit. Don't just stick to traditional fruits; try some new ones as well. Some things you might think are vegetables are really fruit! Try to include at least one pepper, tomato, and apple, along with a squash or cucumber. Avoid seedless varieties.

46

- **Tip:** Bananas do have seeds, but they are very tiny, appearing as little black spots in the center of a banana slice. You can try to count them, but it is not recommended!

- **Tip:** If you dissect a pepper, be sure to wash your hands before you touch your eyes after handling the seeds. Pepper seeds can be spicy and cause a burning sensation! Use a mild pepper variety, such as a bell pepper, if you are very sensitive.

- You may need an adult to help you when cutting the fruit open.

PROCEDURE

Begin to dissect your first fruit, removing the seeds and placing them on a paper towel. *In the fruit, are the seeds arranged in a certain pattern?*

When you are done removing the seeds, count the number of seeds on the paper towel. *How many seeds were in the fruit?*

Tip: If you are dissecting a cucumber or squash, instead of removing the seeds you can try cutting the fruit lengthwise, counting the rows of seeds, and then slicing the fruit the other way to determine how many seeds are in one row. Multiply these two numbers together to get a good approximation of the total number of seeds.

One at a time, continue to dissect each fruit, place the seeds on a paper towel, then count them. Be sure to keep the seeds from different fruits separated.

How many seeds are in each fruit? Which held the most seeds? The least? Did similar types of fruit produce similar numbers of seeds?

How do seeds from different types of fruit look similar or different? In each fruit, were there similar patterns in which the seeds were arranged?

SCIENCE FAIR IDEA

Try this activity again, but use multiple fruit of each type, such as multiple peppers, tomatoes, cucumbers, and squash. *Does the same type of fruit always hold a similar number of seeds, or does the amount vary a lot?*

SCIENCE FAIR IDEA

Is fruit size related to seed quantity? Repeat this activity, but this time use a ruler to measure each fruit before you count its seeds to see if larger fruits tend to produce more seeds than smaller ones. (You can also use a scale to weigh each fruit as an alternative way to measure fruit size.) *Do larger fruits make more seeds?*

EXTRA

Are seedless fruit varieties really seedless? Dissect several different varieties of seedless fruits and look for seeds. *Are "seedless" fruit varieties completely seedless, or do they have fewer seeds than normal? What is the decreased seed productivity of seedless varieties compared with normal varieties on a fruit-to-fruit comparison basis?*

OBSERVATIONS AND RESULTS ··············

Did some types of fruit clearly have more seeds than others? Did the cucumbers, squash, tomato, and pepper have a lot of seeds, easily over 100 each? Did the apple only have a few seeds, no more than 10?

Fruits are divided into three general groups, with the "simple fruits" group making up the majority we encounter. They're formed from one ovary in one of the plant's flowers. As the ovary turns into fruit, different ovary parts become different fruit parts; when fertilized, small structures called ovules become the fruit's seeds—and more fertilized ovules means more seeds! The other two fruit groups are more complex. In "aggregate fruit"—such as raspberries—multiple ovaries fuse on a single flower. In the third group, called "multiple fruit," many ovaries and flowers unite. A pineapple is a good example of a "multiple fruit."

Cucumbers, melons, and squash are simple fruits. (They are part of a fruit type called pepo. These are types of berries) with a firm rind and softer, watery interior. And, as you probably saw, these fruits make many seeds! A zucchini or cucumber can easily have a couple hundred neatly patterned seeds.

Tomatoes, grapes, kiwifruit, and peppers are also simple fruits (technically true berries) with fleshier walls and usually very fluid insides—think of how watery a ripe tomato is! Some, like tomatoes and peppers, can have a couple hundred seeds, whereas others, like kiwifruit, can have several hundred! Citrus fruits are berries (a type called hesperidium) too, with leathery rinds and usually only a few seeds.

Similarly, apples and pears also only have a few seeds (10 at most), but they are not berries—they belong to a different fruit type known as pomes, which have some fruit flesh not made from the flower's ovary but rather from plant tissue near the ovary. It's the same for strawberries.

CLEANUP •

Dispose of the seeds from your fruit or, if you're motivated and curious, look into how you could grow plants from your seeds. You can eat the rest of the fruit or save it for a tasty, healthy snack later!

49

Sweltering Science
Are Rooftop Gardens a Cool Idea?

WILL PLANTS ON A ROOF CHANGE THE BUILDING'S TEMPERATURE? FIND OUT WITH THIS EASY EXPERIMENT.

PROJECT TIME

2 to 3 hours

KEY CONCEPTS

Energy conservation
Temperature
Heat
Plants
Insulation

Have you ever seen a rooftop garden? Around the world, people have transformed some rooftops into living green areas. Besides beauty, rooftop gardens have a number of very visible advantages, including growing (very) local food. How would you like homegrown sky vegetables for dinner or some fresh-cut roof flowers for vases in your house? Rooftop gardens also take carbon dioxide out of the air while releasing breathable oxygen. Chicago's City Hall is one famous building with a rooftop garden. But can rooftop gardens keep your house cooler and lower your energy bill on hot summer days? Try this activity to find out!

51

BACKGROUND

Rooftop gardens, also called living roofs or green roofs, have many advantages, including providing more space for agriculture, adding beauty to a cityscape, and increasing air quality. During photosynthesis, plants remove carbon dioxide from the air and release oxygen that we need to breathe.

On hot summer days, rooftop gardens may also keep buildings cooler than traditional roofs—especially on larger buildings that often have tar and gravel roof surfaces. Because they sit in the direct sunlight for many hours, the temperature of traditional rooftops tends to rise above the actual air temperature. That heat radiates back into the environment, making urban areas much warmer than rural and suburban ones. If you live in a big city or have visited a shopping center with a lot of concrete and buildings during warm months, you might have noticed the temperature difference. When heat is radiated back into the environment from rooftops, an area with many buildings, like a city, can experience an increase in local air temperatures by as much as 5 to 7 degrees! This phenomenon is called the urban heat island effect.

MATERIALS

- Two shoeboxes, photo storage boxes, or 1/2 gallon (1.9 l) cardboard milk cartons. The boxes should be the same size, color, and shape.
- Sod, available at most nurseries or garden supply stores. Alternatively, a small amount of moist soil, some freshly pulled weeds, and tape may be used.
- Exacto knife (and an adult's help when using this tool)
- A sunny spot outside on a hot day
- Thermometer
- Clock or timer

PREPARATION

- Place one of the box's lids (or the side of a milk carton) on the sod. Using the knife, carefully cut around the lid to get a piece of sod the same size as the lid. Adult assistance may be needed to use the knife. Place the cut-out sod piece on top of the box (or on the side of the milk carton).

- If you are using soil and weeds instead of sod, use tape to make a raised perimeter around the edge of the lid, then pour a thin layer of moist soil on the lid (the tape should help contain the soil) and then add several freshly pulled weeds.

- You should now have one box with sod (or soil and weeds) on it, which will represent your rooftop garden house, and one box without anything on it, which will represent your traditional house.

PROCEDURE

On a hot sunny day, put the thermometer in the box with sod on it, close the box, and take it outside.

Place the box in the sunny spot you picked. Leave it in the sun for 30 minutes. (You'll want to test both boxes in the same cloud conditions, specifically when it is sunny and warm out for the entire 30 minutes that each box is outside. If cloud conditions change when you are testing a box, try to retest it again later when it's warm and sunny out.)

When 30 minutes have passed, open the box and quickly read the thermometer. *How hot is it inside the box?*

Put the thermometer in the shade near the box (still outside). After it has adjusted to the shade, read the temperature. *How hot is it in the shade? How does this compare to how hot it was in the box?*

Repeat these steps with the box that doesn't have sod on it. *How hot did it get in the box without sod on it after 30 minutes? How does this compare to how hot it is in the shade, outside of the box?*

Overall, which box was coolest inside, compared to the temperature outside of the box in the shade? *Can you explain your results?*

EXTRA

You could investigate how having a rooftop garden affects a building's temperature over the course of the day by repeating this activity but keeping the boxes outside the entire day and taking measurements throughout the day (including after it gets dark outside) or by using a heat lamp on the boxes to mimic a hot day (and turning the lamp off to mimic the sun going down). *How does the temperature of the boxes change over the course of a day?*

EXTRA

You could try growing your own rooftop gardens for your box houses and explore many variables. *What kinds of plants work best? Does soil depth alter the temperature results?*

EXTRA

You could explore how having a rooftop garden affects how warm a building stays during the winter. To do this, repeat this activity but this time test the boxes on a cooler day (or indoors) and put a layer of ice cubes on top of the boxes. (Cover the boxes first with plastic wrap to keep them dry.) You could alternatively place the boxes on top of a tray of ice (again covered with plastic wrap). *Which box stays the warmest in winter-like conditions?*

OBSERVATIONS AND RESULTS ・・・・・・・・・

Did the box with the "rooftop garden" stay cooler than the plain box?

It's thought that rooftop gardens might be able to diminish the urban heat island effect. Generally, rooftop gardens absorb heat and insulate buildings better than traditional tar and gravel roofs. In this activity, you should have seen this; while both boxes were probably warmer than the temperature in the shade nearby, the box with the sod (or soil and weeds) should have been relatively cooler inside compared to the box without the sod. As an example of how real rooftop gardens can help keep their buildings cool, measurements from the Chicago City Hall building show that on a summer day when the air temperatures were over 90°F (32°C), areas of the roof area covered in black tar rose to a surface temperature of 169°F (76°C), while areas planted with a rooftop garden only rose to 119°F (48°C)—that's a 50-degree difference!

CLEANUP ・・・・・・・・・・・・・・・・・・・・・・

With permission, you can plant your sod somewhere or compost it. Any clean cardboard can be recycled.

Water-Wise
Keep Soil Wet Without Waste

WHEN TO WATER: YOUR SOIL TYPE PLAYS A BIG ROLE IN HOW OFTEN YOU SHOULD WATER PLANTS. HOW? TRY THIS SOGGY SCIENCE ACTIVITY AND FIND OUT!

PROJECT TIME
 60 to 90 minutes

KEY CONCEPTS

Geology
Water-holding capacity
Soil types

In the summer, you might see colorful flowers, fresh tomatoes, and yummy berries in a garden. But who is watering them? Maybe you wonder if they get enough—or too much—water. Should they get water every day, twice a day, or once a week? Should they be soaked or is frequently providing small amounts of water better? Unfortunately, there is no general rule because much depends on the type of soil. In this science activity, you will see how much water soil can hold by practicing with readily available kitchen substitutes for dirt. Once you understand some general principles, you should be better equipped to tackle the real problem of watering wisely.

56

BACKGROUND

Some experts claim U.S. residents use billions of gallons of water outdoors each day. Watering gardens is one contributor to this use. Why is it so difficult to water a garden wisely while protecting plants and avoiding waste?

Ideal watering schedules (how much and how frequently you should water) depend largely on how much water the soil can hold. If the soil cannot hold water well, a more frequently added and smaller amount of water is needed. For soil that can hold water, a less frequent substantial watering schedule is better.

Two factors play a major role in determining the water-holding capacity of soil: its structure—or how big or small the particles in the soil are—and the amount of organic material present. Organic material refers to broken-down plant and animal material. Water loves to cling to organic material, so more of it mixed into the soil allows more water retention. In terms of soil structure, smaller particles have more surface area for the same volume of soil, meaning more area where water can stick. This activity will try out this idea with insoluble dry food. Will grinding up the food allow the same volume of substance to hold more water?

MATERIALS

- Paper towels or kitchen towels to protect your workspace in case of spills
- Four identical glasses (preferably with rather narrow openings so the cone-shaped coffee filters can rest in them)
- Three clean, cone-shaped paper coffee filters
- 1/3 cup measuring cup
- 2/3 cup dried rice, rice meal (or coarsely ground rice), and rice flour (or finely ground rice) (Alternatively, you can use dried corn kernels, cornmeal, and corn flour; or grain berries, bulgur, and wheat flour.)
- A helper
- Water
- A workspace that can tolerate some liquid splashes
- Paper and pen (or pencil)
- Plastic coffee filter cone(s), which can hold your paper filters and help prevent spills (optional)
- Kitchen scale (optional)

57

PREPARATION ·····················

- Protect your workspace with some paper towels or a kitchen towel

- Open a coffee filter and let it rest in the opening of a glass. Repeat with two other filters and glasses. You will have one glass left.

- If you have coffee filter holders available, use them, especially for the dried rice. They will help prevent spills.

- Add 2/3 cup of dried rice in the first filter.

- Add 2/3 cup of rice meal in the second filter.

- Add 2/3 cup of rice flour in the last filter.

PROCEDURE ·····················

- If you have a kitchen scale available, weigh the filters with the dry substances, one at a time. Write down your measurements.

- Look at the three substances: dried rice, rice meal, and rice flour. *How are they similar and how are they different?*

- In a moment you will pour water over these substances. *Which one do you think can hold more water? How could you measure how much water it can hold?*

- Pour 1/3 cup (78 ml) of water over the dried rice. Before you do so, ask a helper to hold the filter up so it does not flip over and spill. If you have a coffee filter holder, this will do the job as well.

- Repeat the previous step, now pouring 1/3 cup (78 ml) of water over the rice meal. Then pour the same amount of water over the rice flour. Observe what happens. *Does water seep through the substances? Why does this happen?*

- Water gets pulled down by gravity. *In the three setups, why does the water not seep through in the same way in the three cases?*

- Pour another 1/3 cup (78 ml) of water over each substance. Be careful; the filter might flip. *Do you think more or less water will seep through this time?*

- Fill the last glass with 2/3 cup (158 ml) of water and place it next to the other glasses. *How could this glass help you discover which substance can hold the most water?*

- After about five minutes, compare how much water ran through the substances in the glasses. Your fourth glass shows you how much water you poured over the substances. *Which glass has the most water? If there is less water in some glasses, where has the water gone?*

- If you have a kitchen scale, weigh each filter with its wet substance. *Are the measurements different from the mass of the dry materials measured in the first step? Which samples gained the most mass? Where is this extra mass coming from?*

ExTRA

If you have compost available, you can measure how adding compost influences the water-holding capacity of soil. For example, you could create a 1:2 compost-rice meal mixture by adding one scoop of compost for each two scoops of rice meal and compare the water-holding capacity of this mixture to that of pure rice meal using the method described in this activity.

ExTRA

Can you measure how much water the soil in your garden or flowerpot can hold? Take a sample of dry soil from the garden or the flowerpot. If the soil is wet, you will need to let it dry before you do the test. Crumble the soil so it is loose and grainy and perform the test from this activity. How much water can 2/3 cup of soil hold? What would happen if, during a watering cycle, you add more water to this soil? Should you let the soil dry out completely before re-watering? How could that influence your watering schedule?

EXTRA

Geologists classify soils into three main types: sand, silt, and clay. Clay has the smallest particles; you might need a microscope to see them. Next comes silt and then sand. *Which type of soil do you expect to hold water best?* If you can find small samples of these types of soil, repeat the experiment with them to test your prediction.

OBSERVATIONS AND RESULTS ••••••••••••

Was the dried rice barely able to hold water whereas the smallest grind retained the most water?

Water runs downward because it is being pulled by gravity. Water needs a surface to cling to in order to overcome gravity and stay in the sample. The more you grind a substance, the smaller the particles in the substance are—and the more total surface there is for water to hold onto.

Soils differ not only in particle size but also in consistency (or what materials comprise them). Still, particle size plays an important role in determining how much water the soil can hold. Sandy soil has a larger particle size; it cannot hold much water and needs frequent smaller doses of water. Silt has smaller particles; its water-holding capacity is ideal for most plants. Clay has tiny particles, so it might retain too much water, causing plants to rot.

Adding organic content (broken-down plant and animal material) to soil not only increases its nutrient content but also improves its water-holding capacity.

CLEANUP ••••••••••••••••••••••••••

Your samples and filters can go into the compost bin. Water your plants with the leftover water.

THE SCIENTIFIC METHOD

The scientific method helps scientists—and students—gather facts to prove whether an idea is true. Using this method, scientists come up with ideas and then test those ideas by observing facts and drawing conclusions. You can use the scientific method to develop and test your own ideas!

Question: What do you want to learn? What problem needs to be solved? Be as specific as possible.

Research: Learn more about your topic and refine your question.

Hypothesis: Form an educated guess about what you think will answer your question. This allows you to make a prediction you can test.

Experiment: Create a test to learn if your hypothesis is correct. Limit the number of variables, or elements of the experiment that could change.

Analysis: Record your observations about the progress and results of your experiment. Then analyze your data to understand what it means.

Conclusion: Review all your data. Did the results of the experiment match the prediction? If so, your hypothesis was correct. If not, your hypothesis may need to be changed.

61

GLOSSARY

absorb: To take in or soak up liquid.

botanist: A scientist who studies plants.

clone: To create a copy of a living thing.

disperse: To spread over a large area.

insulate: To protect something from losing heat or cold.

matter: Anything that has weight and takes up space.

nutrient: A substance in food that helps fuel living things.

organic: Matter that comes from a recently living organism.

particle: The smallest unit of matter.

pesticide: A chemical used to destroy bugs or other organisms that harm plants.

pigment: The natural coloring of a plant.

protect: To keep safe from harm.

radiate: To spread out from a central point.

saturate: To soak with liquid so no more can be absorbed.

substitute: To use something in place of another thing.

thermometer: Device used to read the temperature of an object or living thing.

ADDITIONAL RESOURCES

Books

Jose, Dr. Sarah. *Trees, Leaves, Flowers & Seeds: A Visual Encyclopedia of the Plant Kingdom.* New York, NY: DK Publishing, 2019.

Morlock, Rachael. *Makerspace Projects for Understanding Plant Science.* New York, NY: PowerKids Press, 2021.

Raij, Emily. *What Do Plants Need to Survive?* North Mankato, MN:Pebble, 2022

Websites

Discovery Education
sciencefaircentral.com

Exploratorium
www.exploratorium.edu/search/science%20fair%20projects

Science Buddies
www.sciencebuddies.org/science-fair-projects/project-ideas/list

Science Fun for Everyone!
www.sciencefun.org/?s=science+fair

Videos

Botany: Botany Basics
wqed.pbslearningmedia.org/resource/botany-basics/botany-basics/

Plant Families
wqed.pbslearningmedia.org/resource/thnkgard.sci.ess.plantfam/think-garden-plant-families/

INDEX